"Death and its horror, whether we ignore it or not, await us all. Jessica Bebenek's brilliant poems are a burning light just ahead of us, and we follow each page with a new sense of breathing. I love this book; it gave me a beautiful living frame for the great vanishing trick of life, and I want to buy a copy for everyone I love!"
—CAConrad, author of *Listen to the Golden Boomerang Return*

"In these poems, tending to loss and to life is kaleidoscopic—sorrow and gratitude brightly shine, blur together, transform into other emotions, other perspectives. Attentiveness, here, is enthralling and deeply felt. The language is deftly calibrated to the life-changing and to the life-giving. Startling imagery ('feet swelled beyond shoes') and hard-won insight ('We accept love/now knowing/it will leave us.') rattle and soothe. Jessica Bebenek is a dazzlingly gifted poet who has written a book that echoes and lingers."
—Eduardo C. Corral, author of *Guillotine*

"In *No One Knows Us There*, Jessica Bebenek lays bare death processes, grief, and resilience with a documentarian's eye. Her lyrics sing not only of 'the mundanity of being left behind' but also desire, and the beauty there is to be found in entropy. She writes, 'if bent rings and broken chains can/transmute, deform…so I can/draw experience into my fractures.' A truly compelling debut."
—Liz Howard, author of *Letters in a Bruised Cosmos*

"[*No One Knows Us There*] brings the whole chaos of youthful mourning to light in episodes of drama, insight, and humour. Its achievement is one of poetry's most difficult: to raise despair to an aesthetic act by honouring, and not merely decorating, its core of personal tragedy."
—Bronwen Wallace Award for Emerging Writers jury citation

No One Knows Us There

Poems

Jessica Bebenek

Book*hug Press
Toronto 2025

"Atoms" words by Theo Hilton, music by Nana Grizol © 2010 by Theo Hilton. All Rights Reserved. Used with permission.
"Real Death" words by Phil Elverum, music by Phil Elverum © 2017 by P.W. Elverum & Sun. All Rights Reserved. Used with permission.

Library and Archives Canada Cataloguing in Publication
Title: No one knows us there / Jessica Bebenek.
Names: Bebenek, Jessica, author.
Identifiers: Canadiana (print) 20240524233 | Canadiana (ebook) 20240526430
   ISBN 9781771669399 (softcover)
   ISBN 9781771669405 (EPUB)
Subjects: LCGFT: Poetry.
Classification: LCC PS8603.E3969 N6 2025 | DDC C811/.6—dc23

The production of this book was made possible through the generous assistance of the Canada Council for the Arts and the Ontario Arts Council. Book*hug Press also acknowledges the support of the Government of Canada through the Canada Book Fund and the Government of Ontario through the Ontario Book Publishing Tax Credit and the Ontario Book Fund.

Book*hug Press acknowledges that the land on which we operate is the traditional territory of many nations, including the Mississaugas of the Credit, the Anishnaabeg, the Chippewa, the Haudenosaunee, and the Wendat peoples. We recognize the enduring presence of many diverse First Nations, Inuit, and Métis peoples, and are grateful for the opportunity to meet and work on this territory.

for Alan & Scott

One

Two

Death is real.
Someone's there and then they're not.

—Mount Eerie, "Real Death"

Hospice

Here is what happened: I took a walk.
In the sense that I walked out of the room
to the kitchen, got a coffee. Talked to a man
who made small cakes, had daughters my age,
liked to shop at a store on Queen. He volunteered
to reduce my pain, to populate a house
of appropriate sorrow.

I took another walk. I walked to a secondary
room housing relatives. We discussed the affairs
of the day: initials, legalities, beneficiaries, moving dates,
whether a body is burned with or without clothes on.
A newspaper sat on a glass coffee table. It housed
an image of a man swinging a long, smooth
piece of wood.

The third and final walk took place outside.
In it, I carried the coffee, looked at the sky,
considered the feeling of floating over the edge
of existence while one of us takes their time falling.
The garden was beautiful. Well cared for. The sun was rising.
When a father opened a window, leaned out,
it was with a cinematic quality. It was life.
There descended a condition of calm urgency
revealed to me in the bareness of its clatter.

I lied. There was a fourth walk, but it confused itself
with heartbeat, the brain instructing the lungs to pump
within a vacuum. The feet finding sheets of stone beneath
themselves and these stones leading

around the side of the house, through several doors,
an accommodating hallway,
back into the room of the poem's origin.
It was a room containing all the bodies I knew
in varying states of decomposition.

Forestalled Decomposition for Public Display

Under the basement ceiling
the embalmer works his trade.
He keeps in mind: sanitation,
preservation, presentation.
He removes the clothing,
the underthings, discreetly
reveals the bodies, turgid
and angular. From behind
the surgical mask, he aspirates
fluids and gases from the torso,
relieves pressure. He tends
to outstanding blemishes,
potential points of leakage
stuffed with cotton.
He reunites cranial fragments,
unfurling the scalp in a single sheet.

The embalmer moves
through the throaty pumping
backdrop of chemicals:
formaldehyde, methanol, etc.
Disinfectants and antiseptics
enter via the jugular.
The slow, downward
growth of a tree.
He massages the fluids
through clenched veins,
grasps flesh, works shaggy
skin around its bone,

thick wrists and bare thighs.
He pinches the thin
wrinkles of infant fingers,
furrowed as a question.

The embalmer applies
scented oils to the skin
and runs his fingers through hair.
He paints the lips neutral
with a fine, squirrel hair brush.
He sets the lids of the eyes
to sleep—denarii, crossed
stitches, adhesive gels.
He blows on them
with concentrated breath.
Imagine the ventilation
system sucking souls
through the silkscreen.

Above, beating wings
enact an invisible, perpetual
motion: they force air to the ground.
Down here, there are no lies.
The sky is no longer a place.

This Is the Morning of a Meaningless Sparrow at the Window

This is not you.
This is wincing,
a shrunken man, flesh
loosed from the bone.
This is a body letting go.
This is the stench
of lungs rotting and exiting
spore by spore through the mouth.
This is existence
loosening its ties.

These are quiet nurses,
these are shaken breaths, gasps, all of us
measuring voids between your choked inhalations.
The blunt necessity of dry mouth serum. These are
comatose moans, these are comforted cries.
The manipulation of your limp limbs after they change your palliative
     adult diaper.
This is the curl of the toes, their grey-blueing.
My attempt to grip the ground,
your thin calves, your slack thighs.
This is my hand placed on the skin covering your ribs, your chest
in the dark, indigo walls, opening
this body, the night cracking. This is silent
crying through a room filled with bodies
snores this is the closing of a door these illuminated faces
heads buried in phones your body
buried at the centre of it all

This is the morning
of a meaningless sparrow at the window.
The men are crying. They are holding each other.
Here is the attempt to close your mouth. We were lied to.
This was not a slow slip. There was pain.

04:05

I remember
words and their coming uncomplicated

Winter oozing clouds on the afternoon
pastel walls lecture of passing hours I remember

happiness People said goodnight to me
before they went to sleep Our choices:

foreign languages rumbling through a clumsy mouth
Remember

when it all just worked
We hadn't conceived of

the breakdown no consolation no plot just
stop This is the end and I didn't know it would be

not missing you not happy just a dark
room with a mouth in it just my own

inability
Remember when we were so

Remember That's it.

On the Night of the Morning
My Grandfather Died

we got shit-faced. Crawled through the pubs of that town
with its illusion of smallness. The moon and its illusion of light. On that oh
so symbolically bitter October night, my father and I drank
like mourning and drinking are what we'd been born to do.
Everything about us
dragged itself home long before we could.
      His soul nestled somewhere deep
      in his hanging mouth.
      His body naked, maybe
      already burning.
We forgot
finances, bartenders' names, basic geography,
all immediate and inherent dangers.

Tumbling out the long way
home, we followed train tracks over water.
The streets' orange fading to deep blue deluge
beneath, that drop—
he tried to dare me to be afraid.
There was no approaching whistle, no distant light,
no hole big enough to lose anything.
Only this silly business of time
opening its coat to us, bloated
with existence, each time a body's rocked
against mine, our limitless love, reckless grasp on life, my foot
plunging between boards, because I am full, heavier than the train
with the single light of my approach, heavy with empties rattling through me

that pull my whole body through the spaces between splintered grains,
    push my whole body to the water, to the rocks,
and stop. Hold me while I fall. My small
body in a warm lap. With infinite tenderness,
prepare my breakfast. Recall my name.

But there is no fall.
We went home.
Chose one board
and then another,
one street and walked down it,
screeching with the thing
that made us.

Repeat Directive

to pick at your lips like your grandmother
picked incessantly at her lips

to be trapped by the house
like your grandmother, trapped and ever-waiting

for what. to split down the middle
like her nails ever-splitting still picking

and you are not done yet
this winter is still coming to know this

to wake nightly
convinced there is a right way to think

and it will lead you out to safety to pluck
a certain future between your thumb and index finger

and blow to let go there it goes
on the air with the rest of your life

The Way Fish Drown

My grampa died gasping, mouth open
to gulp whatever life had yet to bring him.
Turns out it's true: the toes curl, blue, point

back to their beginning.
It's just the body that leaves.
I heard they burned it after putting it in his clothes.

Skin webs over ribs, thins and hangs
beneath the eyeholes. Death
is a full stop we lace

into chronology, tie bows
on the articles of the living. File
his face into some subcategory.

I can't tell you what he learned
around back of a Regina farmhouse,
the intention of the cries

he replayed before sleep; what terrors gurgled out
his lips from the bottom of the prairie sky.
Whatever we keep for ourselves.

His feet swelled beyond shoes, then slippers,
became powdery-white oysters sucked
from their shells. Magenta abalones

of his eyelids sunk closed.
Muscles slackened.
Urine stained the side of the bed.

These homes hold us until they slip
from the crease they cleaved into.
Sinews snap from the low-tide rock face

as each memory flicks a moment
its newly opened nerve to the salt air.
We all get dragged

by the next wave to obscurity—
another drowned fish, another
wreck's rib half-buried.

Deer

I wanted to write a poem about a deer
but by the time I got around to it,

it was probably already dead.
I guess that makes this an elegy.

I watched it through the chain-link fence,
my fingers clawed around the diamond outline of its metal-

etched body darting through the crooks of electrical towers.
No, he was a stag, big, with antlers, and with ink-

deep eyes I could look into and I would feel them
like he was looking into me and not bleating with his eyes shut.

He kept reeling around on his two back legs and his soft browns looked grey
like the grass and the pile of concrete cylinders to the right. His nose kept

spraying out puffs of hot sleet and there was all this steam
coming off his back. I could see the meat

pulsing around his bones. I wanted to call someone to catch
him, help him, or— I wanted to grab someone's

arms hard and tell them he needed help. I wanted
to press my palms flat on his wet, shaking body.

I wanted to help him. Instead, I watched him smack
his hooves off a path of broken asphalt slabs

and disappear down the drooping rows
of thick black cables

The Garden

The mug didn't drop.
No, not so
dramatic. I was taking a turn

when the call struck
through the window. My not

dispassionate response,
temperate steps on flag-
stone, in the front door.
But I've told you this before.

The response, the call,
blunt edge of rationale,
disbelief and its rise
like a wall. Uniform

bricks for eyes in the starved faces
which turned from the corpse.

They'd called it. Watches
stopped precisely as I'd
twisted head from stem,
shifted floral stoneware from left
to right and set my bowels
in the grass
where they could warm in the morning light.

The beings in the room
busied themselves about their tasks,
taking the hand in their hands,

the forehead to their mouths.
I missed the rattle
and was not told
how it passed with the blessing
of a coffee break.

Life fumbled its way through him,
clutched lungs, his breath ripped
out (you'll remember) like a panicked stag
and I won't bore you
anymore with bleak and beautiful woods,
softly falling snow, its gracious crush
because I can't fucking write these poems anymore.

*

Probably somewhere a squirrel is smelling a flower or something.
Somewhere in the past I described my existence as fingers straining to
    touch a brick wall.

This blood-red gem
forces my hand
for the last time.

Somewhere in the garden a squirrel
lay dead. Imagine this body
on the path in the flower bed:

the soft sway of its tail
in the breeze, the morning light
in its glossy almond eyes.

Wonder how life left it
so intact.

Hic Iacet Sepultus

Haworth Parsonage

It was the father who came to divine
the trickle of thaw from their home
above the graveyard. Picture
perilous, sloping country. They lived

their lives in colour just three weeks of the year.
Think thickets, brambles, hills that hoard
lakes in their crags. Note buckshot
littering the old steeple. *Verbi Dei Minister.*

Here is where starts the rain's slow slip
through decomposing bodies layered on bodies.
Those allotted time to ramble were not easily charmed
and survived, at least, to teach the children

not shitting to death in the street
of the speckled markings of *Muscicapa striata,*
how to spot a common lacewing.
Pleasant as cobblestone may be,

it's no reprieve from diseased entrails.
No replacement for porcelain bowls; the pale
lean legs of writing desks; petite quills or
pellets of sealing wax, their gilt boxes.

Look, if you lived below the church,
you drank water filtered through corpses.
Even the cemetery cat kicked the bucket,
plucking nuthatches who plucked spores

from tainted lichen. They took turns
attending the pungent services. Rot
piled on the problem. Between classes,
walks, attending to correspondences,

they prayed. Chaste bodies still
keep to themselves in stone, confirming
the souls of those who live

through the thaw. Spring is an ancient word meaning
dead birds, sweet God,
their crooked corpses are everywhere.

Trinity Dream

I knew I should not look back at the corpse,
but I looked back at the corpse and I cried.
My father pulled me away.

We had to prepare for the long trip ahead.
My father lay in the snow where he died.
I knew I should not look back at the corpse

to watch my father rear above it, fists striking
ground with the fury of staying alive.
My father pulled me away

from my father who came back only to still
his fears: he could not have committed the crime.
I knew I should not look back at the corpse.

When I looked, my screams gagged, some feminine
choking; the kindling-snap of space, of time.
My father pulled me away

to finish the job of his grieving.
He could not. Nor could I.
I knew I should not look back at the corpse.
My father pulled me away.

On Melancholia

When it came, true, it *was* the most beautiful sight.
Finally submersed from all sense, we turned our hands outward,
supplicant, open to impact. Our face blown tight with fortune.
Children whittled magic caves of refuge into our shelled heart. For them,

we scrawled across tissue paper rising around flame, *we will live forever.*
And we believed it. How could we stop.
Inaction bloomed sweetly, one million sticky swarms crawled
their felted legs across the blossom of our soul; full nebulae

burning magenta and cerulean across an infinite, lifeless sky.
We'd stood in a thick grey sweater in the background of every picture,
holding each other's hand. Up front, the fearful face of a mother,
tears bathing feet at a prophetic screen. Her pacifier:

a twig, spiral of wire, leather watchband.
She didn't understand movement in its futility,
defined by the law of its constant spin.
We bathed ourselves in that light, naked, penetrating

porous logic, blindness and its childish blessings,
inescapable terror. Its turn and shrug at the edge of existence.
When we died, our hair and fingertips lit like votives,
smoked themselves back to their gaseous existence.

No one missed us. No birds chirping. We returned to our stable.
No one gathered where the terrace used to be,
sipped red, sang us a sad, sad song. Just that little
melancholia, the last light left on.

The Flight

we found the minuscule pockets of sound indistinguishable
from the IMAX experience the domed vinyl
panelled like Sheetrock outliving each monarch

in gorgeous CGI flight   they make the yearly trip
to Mexico cyclical the accent of simulated *whooshes*
against their delicately panelled wings   we learned

a full migration costs three lives observed time exerted
in the slow birth from a picnic table chrysalis   first stretch
of their new wings to the sun a promise of transience

we found them roosting in Angangueo layering
the pine needles thicker than fur bodies bursting
a firestorm spiralling themselves uncontrollably

into the sky coating us in a fine mist
nestled in the cool heart of the theatre
we watched the monarchs lurch their way up

to the jet streams coast on them for days
the survivors knowing better than to fight
against the currents and risk exhaustion

Cosmos

O Neil deGrasse Tyson, I need you
more than words can say. To tell me again
of our slow seep through generations,
our transient companionship. Fill me again
with beer and then weed and then food
and then a little more weed. You know
what I need. Superior knowledge slams
against me and *crack* I am less than
a second, less than quantifiable worth,
caloric nourishment, fidelity.
                              There are so
many things, Neil deGrasse Tyson, rushing
away from us at exponentially increasing speeds
and only one thing rushing toward us.
The more I listen, the more I imagine
I could understand you. Neil, I have so many ideas.
What's your mailing address?

The World Without

I watch the world decline   The weeds survive
The pitting on a blade

To encapsulate as a worm encapsulates earth
While encapsulated by earth

This year I get fucked in the face   This year I bleed all over a man
And I am not sorry and he does not want me to be

A web   A spiderweb   A can of Coke caught in a spiderweb
A harness on a cat   Do not let any of this excruciating be in vain

Have you considered the beauty of being
Absolutely worthless   Have you considered the freedom

I put my feet on the grass
Under the asphalt   Where does it go

Even knowing change to be the way of all life
And still   Even knowing this

I longed to stop forever
In a way that is not death

Just let me be a table lamp   a lap   a tea
My mind buried as a cottage in honeysuckle   Just let me be

Two-Night Stand

I thought the hole in me was a body
waiting to be filled. So I slipped you in,
your voice low on the couch, a pearl
in your mouth, and I dove.

I rode you to a finish, kiss
to close your lineless lips. What stopped
was not our hearts, not time:
the fraction of my sight that caught
the space between our skins.

The Future of Condo Living

It's the beginning of winter and still
the city opens itself down to the base
of its square-ruled throat. Sturdy
ramps of sand for the dozers, matchsticks
of iron beams jutting from the suggestion of structure.

You kiss with acceptable pacing
against the edge of craters, press
to their frail hemlines.
It becomes impossible to determine scale; the image
of a warning sign, boozy fingers curling around chain.
The irony of staring into a massive, night-filled hole.

The body comes as a shock. Its presence
in sudden teeth, crags of shoulders. Torso
bald in the light, table lamp on the floor, shaken
game of explanations.
Skin darkens remarkably in areas.

You will spend the night under a pilled sheet
dreaming out possible mornings—
balconied one bedroom plus den
and the view; a cloud bank of Pekingese
rising to greet you. How wholly
unremarkable to be in each other's lives.

Future venue of your waking: a bedsheet curtain's
drooping eyelid, cracked window,
a back to put your hand on,
its unremarkable absence at the door.

And the night, still here, will finish
taking off your shirt. Eyes graciously close.
A person's head between your legs, mild absence of panic.
Your body on its back, being rocked slowly
up and down.
This moment
is no one you have ever loved, ever touched.
The whole city rushing suddenly into a single sensation
and leaving you there. A kiss on the night's empty street.

The Future

Here is the moment   when you leave

without leaving   You don't say a thing

You don't flick   two fingers at my brim

Here we are   You are not saying

Well.   in a matter-of-fact tone

You are not   hanging my hand on your doorknob

This is the couch   on which we are sitting

Bed on which   we are touching

Kitchen   in which we are eating

We just lie   down

Press our knees   into each other's pits of knees

We never try again   Forget each smell which crept

toward its source   which called us home

These months   of hearing nothing

                     but the moon's white silence

Light streams in the window

                              because I told it to

Second-Hand Elegy

for Ben

I keep trying to get to the other
side of your story, make anything bare
as it felt, falling before me
last summer on your aunt's roof.

You came from here,
then Nova Scotia,
then came back here,

told me every stick-and-poke
ropes its maker,

every kitchen chair you've sat in,
to your skin.

I brought the beer.
I got it around the corner.

You spoke about that stained street
we still walk on.

Your explication so practised
it paused the cars below us,

and the leaves, and the sun

in its frivolity, burning my chest.

Each time two blunt forms collide,

one succeeds in the other's destruction.

We learned this.

When we touch now in public

it's polite with a lightness

tinged by our letting go.

Trust

I'm waiting for the time when it will feel
like I never lived this life,
never had to.

From wherever I am, I will
send word like a golden thread,
roll an unravelling ball through time
toward myself.

And nothing ever does begin like nothing ever ends.
Ask every atom in your body and they're sure to tell you
"Friend, I'm old as time and older still
and you are made of everything you love, eat, feel, or kill.
I will outlive you and forgive you and be just a baby still."

—Nana Grizol, "Atoms"

Hospice

I draped the mirror, not
out of respect for you
but because I couldn't stand to look at myself

propped or lying, reading, writing—which is
another kind of lying
Eating chickpea cookie pie or nothing

homemade Luna bars or nothing
Who can I trust to be honest
about the things I did

after you left? Surely no one less
than me, some girl
in dank fox fur at a basement apartment party

living like one long exhale, the release
of my hand from the neck
of a bottle, the bottle hitting the floor

Lowering myself slowly
into danger like a scalding bath
Sending nudes to a former professor until

he confessed
he had something like a wife
—the danger of not feeling afraid

Straight weeks smothered
under the wet wool blanket of a white sky
gouging at the back of my throat

—Why go back here?
These days, I feel ecstasy

Well, no. But I feel peace
Chris brings me coffee on the steps
then leaves me alone

to the reviving qualities of quiet
When he says
let's order from the good Thai place tonight

I let my heart leap! a conspiratorial grin
I am a cat being patted in the lap of my life
No one bothers me here, not even memories

tracing like the tepid washrag over your sagging arm flesh
pressed to your twitching lips your parched tongue like a mollusc
—No

I give only what I have
I take only what I need
I leave everything behind

When I was sixteen, I paused in my plastic Loblaws smock
about to spend ten hours standing in one place and considered
throwing myself from the top of the stairs. I'd done it before

and lived.
But of course I didn't
I stood still, handed people their change, wiped down the till

It took years to build the courage to fall again

to bust my knee leaving the karaoke bar on Christmas
in platform boots, to sprain my ankle
biking to A---'s at midnight after D-----'s at nine

I have given over my body to not have to feel
suffered to muffle my own suffering
And now, muffling joy

with feminist cross stitches
hand-sewn upcycled handkerchiefs
homemade vegan shepherd's pie

I have tied myself to life by the leash of mundanity
The mundanity of being left behind
This is a place of love where you go to die

whatever you need for the pain and
people compensated or obligated
to wipe the shit from your genitals
No

Life is not a place I've come to recover
climb enlightenment one rung at a time
or otherwise convince myself of this

upward mobility
but a place to pass through
if I'm lucky, with some comfort

Where are you right now?
You were never promised more
than what you got

Here and elsewhere, people suffer
Where are you right now?
Think back. Think around

Time exists not as a river, but a pond
in which we float

with all the other stories

and I am so grateful
for having floated into you
before you dispersed

I'm sure you heard at some point
how the human body's cells shed and renew completely
every seven years

The antiseptic ablutions
of the final hallway—that room—have passed
through my blood, the last

infused cells rubbed off on a hand towel
how unceremoniously we redistribute how difficult
now to make our way back to humus—but, no

Today I am
seven years after your death
flipping my scaffold like a mattress

I will be totally new

Trust

When someone tells me
this will all have been worth it.
Yes and no. I mean,
this will all have been.

I Was Conceived Under a Chemo Moon

Gratitude toward the houseplants, shame
                for what they must endure
        the hoya repotted and ever-hanging
                        above my creaking bed, its sway
They've outlived me since the day
                  my mother found their shoots reaching
        from his mother's mantel
                  In that sunny bungalow
beneath the power lines I appeared
                  a twinkle in my father's irradiated eye
        My mother had sent herself across the ocean
                      to watch the cells proliferate in her
lover's neck knowing
              their order is not our order
        I was the wink in the nurse's eye
                  as she explained the perks of chemotherapy
Waves radiated through the new life which filled him
            as first he, then I, filled her
        Gratitude toward the parents for keeping it up
                fulfilling their end
        of the evolutionary pact. Shame
for what they must endure—having a child
              like me, offshoot of their reaching, witness
        to the sway of beds and their humans predating me
                  every cell which brings my cells into being
and holds them here
            for a moment
        before exhaling

On the Night of the Morning

when I stroked

your arm with the tips

of my dragging fingers

and you

gasped

purred, the secret

small hairs under your

pale bicep pimpling

rising

to meet me like the sun

glistening

across my bed

over Parc du Père-Marquette

on that night

you returned to me

while I slinked

fingers

over sweating glass

on the crowded *terrasse*

talked a summer

of Turkish ruins with Uma

in the absence

of you, glancing off

I felt

all my living, every posture

mutely drawing you to-

ward me.

And

you

                              minced
                        into that kitchen
                                  glistening still
                        with exertion
                  and whoever's
            glitter slicked onto you
                  at La Plante
      Moving toward you
                  across the crowded kitchen, walls
                                          pimpling
                        with condensation
            our breath overflowing
      passing you fragrant
      gin over ice
from the teeming counter
                  I threatened
            to drag the tip
                  of my tongue across
            your saline neck
            your temple
                        I threatened
            with the tips
      of my fingers glancing
                  off yours
      across the soak-
                  ing wet cup
      I promised
      with my eyes
                  rising
                        to meet yours

Heroic Medicine

When a man had shattered himself beyond rational
repair, those who loved him would feed him

henbane, slip him into a coma deep enough to cut
through his pulpy forearm, dig bone shards from the slush

and fill the hollow with a branch of trembling
aspen. All for the slimmest possibility

of his waking. Like the body which skitters
toward the edge of mortality to achieve stasis,

I have this really bad habit. It's called heterosexuality
and it snaps my neck around in the effort not to break

eye contact with our guide as he slips his fingers up
supple red willow. He explains how a firm limb

was slipped into the remaining soft sockets
of marrow; his half-smile cocked as I cringe.

It takes years for a body to envelop, dissolve
whatever hard thing was put in them while they slept,

forget their way back to their first sturdy knowledge.

Later, I get to the door by the time he returns from wiping
himself off, pulling up my leggings as I remind myself

it's a choice I make, not to disturb the deeply sleeping,
to protect them from the knowledge that nothing grows firm

as the future they'd imagined.
It's said the shock would kill them.

The Place You Leave and the Place You Return To

I once kept a mini-fridge in my bedroom;
that's how holed-up my heart has been.

The eyes of the future are looking back to us
and they are praying. Know, one day, you will

be forced into everything: generosity, nakedness;
a bird who shapes her home

pressing her breast to the walls
a thousand times.

The Garden

The earth inside me wonders about Neanderthals

Had they been instructed yet
on how everything needs me

to be a part of itself to be complete

Or did they think of Chris's lips
murmuring against mine

in bedside light
as he digs himself into sleep

Or how everything public is sacred

how everything I push out of myself
and try to bury remains

The paradox of each deer's brain
holding exactly enough fat to preserve their own skin—

I can't tell you if Neanderthals saw symmetry
in how my knees curled up to my chest in the womb

only that they knew this to be a fitting way
to deliver one another back into it

The Island

I do the laundry so that all is clean
until tomorrow. Here again

in imperfect future
life just goes on

Squatting by the bookshelf

then going to where Chris naps
in the evening on the couch

I stroke his face, his powdery cheek
before he gets up again

to make tomorrow's lunches, wipe down
the counter, replace the Velcro on a boot
before bed

and slowly blinking, his eyes
open to me. Smiling he groans

a question. Of the present moment:
what is happening

Only this and nothing more
then only this again

Nothing

Are you a river
Or nothing?
A tunnel
Or nothing?
You have to tell me
Or I won't know
But I am only joking
If you are not a river
Or a tunnel
Then you are
The snow
Or the protruding plant stalks
Or the huge hidden marsh
We can't ever be nothing
No, not even you
Who has become
Somehow
Everything
How did you do that?

Mountain Theorem

The mathematical theoretician said, if
no one proves my work, it doesn't exist.
The thin films composing his legacy:
individual crystals of salt which form
between layers of the earth's opus.

One, two, three, four, five elk formed before him,
aware and regardless of his gaze.
Elk exist. They eat the grass because
grass exists. He saw it.

How like a poet to stare at one thing
their whole life and for it to be of absolutely
no consequence to the world. How like the elk
to eat, to continue to live.

Moths

They flutter around   trapped

     in the papermaking studio

I won't ever destroy them

     for being

         as it is in their nature to be

They could eat everything I have created

             I would still be here

             I would remain

Snake

You can imagine them as the Great Circle of History:
figurative, unhinged throat opening for their tail,
tucked safely away in some lair beneath bedrock.
That is, until one stops, turns to look

                               right at you.

You can decide to stifle anticipation, the leak
of teeth, hiss of scale to scale as they tighten
in the ever-moment before strike, or you can admit
the realization: someone so other would not decline
their instinct to harm you, to survive.

You can remember that you are the mouse
stiff-limbed, half-submerged in throat, or
a snake is just a mouse gone chthonic, grown
maladapted to extinction.
Twelve million years later

                          a periwinkle tongue
smells your aura, lidless eyes frosted by blindness
take you in in ways you are unevolved to know.
Through open pores of snout, the ambrosian core of you
is revealed:

                   You must open yourself to fear.

The Way Fish Drown

So, what if I switched tactics? I could try
telling the truth for a change.
I could say, simply,
he was a kind person.

Not a body. Or not
only. He was not
the fluids that leaked from him.

He left me so much
more than his remains.

The truth, then:

I loved him.
I was loved

by
him.
It never gets easier than that.

His final words: *Goodbye, sweetheart*
as I stroked back his thin hair.
How, even now,
when Chris calls me *sweetheart*,

my chest cracks open just a little more,
lets in a little more light.

Where did you leave me?

Where did you leave me?   In the dust of a vast desert steppe.

Where did you leave me?   In an expanse, so that you might create a path.

Where did you leave me?   In the nail care aisle of the good Shoppers.

Where did you leave me?   Nowhere and with a great horn at your lips.

Where did you leave me?   With the largest embroidery hoop you own, empty and grasped like a steering wheel.

Where did you leave me?   I did not leave you.

Where did you leave me?   In a garden filled with vine leaves draping from arbours.

Where did you leave me?   In the Koreatown grappa bar across from the KFC.

Where did you leave me?   At the great stone doors to the underworld with a large brass cymbal in each hand.

Where did you leave me?   In the back-corner room of the palliative care home.

Where did you leave me?   That is where I found you.

Where did you leave me?   At the edge of the bonfire at noon so you might witness how even heat casts a shadow.

Where did you leave me?

At the Queen and Spadina McDonald's at 3 a.m.

Where did you leave me?

Raw, cut-out for nothing but want.

Where did you leave me?

In an open secret, not knowing every opening is a wound.

Where did you leave me?

Without blue-blockers on, without a hat, without fingerless gloves.

Where did you leave me?

At a highway bus stop in the late-capitalist wastelands of Mississauga.

Where did you leave me?

With a child who turns upward from her drawing and says *this is a mechanism for repelling love.*

Where did you leave me?

Fingering the edge of your own socket-shaped heart.

Where did you leave me?

I did not leave you.
Stop this.

When I left, you

alchemized, became an altar, sacrifice and worshipper.

When I left, you

held the drum in your own still hands.

When I left, you

felt my love resound like one long note within you which could not sound while crowded by the chatter of living.

When I left, you

had everything you needed to survive. And so you did.

The Box

God is outside

Visions poke holes through

                             the top for air

Death folds down

                         every side of the box

Exposes Us

              like steam

                           to There.

Kintsugi

My friend, the astrogeologist, explained:
> there is a finite amount of gold
> on this planet; enough only, when liquid,
> to fill a regulation Olympic pool.

> When you break, you are guaranteed
> never to come back together as you were,
> only mend into a whole
> with seams displayed.

So, if bent rings and broken chains can
transmute, deform...so I can
draw experience
into my fractures...and still

I will not become the gold, nor
ever me again. Only me now
and now

> and now:
>> chimeral—
a thing of many things—

> a finite being—

>> a time-fused-together being—

> a burst and blended being—

Ragged!—

> Imperfect!—

Yes!—

>> Ever-new...

Raccoons

I love them

            They are little critters

      who creep

         around at night

keeping me

       company

           We are in love

          with what everyone else

      calls trash

We wash

      our stinky rat

           paws to watch

    the dirt swirl

        remake

Love as an Instinct

As I sat on the boat launch's rotting timber, the evening sun shining in sheets
through clouds like a postcard of God, I watched a single loon, smooth
and dark-headed, bobbing with two fuzzy chicks so small they disappeared
behind waves torn up by the wind.

As I watched, they tipped back their glossy head to the sky and called out a
steady siren, a wailing bark across the lake, and listened as the reply, a perfect
echo, grew each time louder, then visible as their partner landed and, with a
great slapping splash and stretch of their speckled wings across the coarse face
of the lake, rejoined.

One and then the other, and then together, they laughed, tossing back and
shaking their shining heads, the haunting chime of their bells in tandem now
ringing over the silent, teeming, sun-capped lake.

When they each rose from their dives, hunting weeds or minnows, I don't
know, and mouthed them, each, to their chicks in easy motions, then down
again for more—who, then, disguised this love as an instinct?

Who looked away from the broad, obvious surface of the lake and cited
simply *hormonal secretion*? As if the loons were oblivious to why they sang or
hunted, or as if we aren't. As if our love is anything more than an impulse, a
series of actions—a calling-out, a laugh, a bringing of mouth to mouth.

The Nature Problem

If I were to lie to you, I would say that nature
is a poet; that whatever nature produces is poetry.

I have watched the skin wrenched neatly from a single
source, with a single cut, from the back of a jackrabbit

in a Liz Howard poem.
Whose is that? Not my satisfaction

at watching the eagle plummet and rise again
with what is nearly a corpse

in its talons. Mary Oliver and repulsion
bringing me right to the lips of what I desire.

But no, nature would never stoop so low
as to produce a work of art. Look at them

out there, not looking at you.

No, only a poet is a poet, glancing away
from their life to coax something else,

something better to wrench through,
determining, all the while, *Yes,*

I trust, this must be exhilaration.
What stuff of life, finally, at hand.

Pet Snail

And again, tomorrow,
   we move smoothly into another
year. While my husband
   and his children sleep
in our beds, I am lying
   five blocks away on my studio floor.
There is something wrong
   with me, a deficit in the heart,
unable to withstand
   their presence, unyielding
attention to me, their attention
   to my attention to them and on and on.

In my heart, I am a pet snail in a mason jar
   cheesecloth rubber-banded to the mouth, crunching
nearly inaudibly on a piece of parboiled carrot.
   Or I am a snail
in a non-place, non-pet, free
   to call myself by whatever is my name.
Or it is okay to be alone, to desire,
   or to desire a desire which
somewhere, somehow, tilts off the edge of longing.

   Here, I read my little books
and what I do not learn there, I look to
   in the pale blue creviced eyelid of a pigeon
as they clean, stutteringly, into their wing fold.

That is how
everything is—the truth of it;
          menacing violet light of city night,
my head on plastic slabs
          pasted with pictures of wood,
and beyond the balcony, bare upper branches waving
          at the inside thought.

The End

And what will I do if
at the end of all this
I am not led by the hand
to understanding?

Well, you don't have to do
a single thing with your life
but wait by the window
and wonder

how you have been so mistaken

There is no end-of-all-this
Your one brief light flashes
amidst the billion, billion sparks

as the Universe rises,
dizzied with expanse,
and tumbles forward
into Creation

This Is the Morning of a Meaningless Sparrow at the Window

You lay me down on the couch and finally
I unfasten. It's just the three of us tonight,
myself and you and the moon,

her little laughing face held safe as she bobs
above your shoulder in the glimmering sky
grown clear of the day's storm.

We walked, watched clouds crown and darken
in the echo of the office park's walls,
a blustering chunk of cement

laid out wide and flat as river rock, the sky
sliding from planes of steel and glass. You called this beauty.
I wondered whether cruelty doesn't call out to us just the same

with the temptation to surrender and be subsumed.
This is my first apocalypse, not yours. You understood
what you saw as you watched the towers fall,

felt real loss, real death
at your wife's change of heart,
your own solitude.

Now we wear masks even outside
to protect each other from something invisible,
something so small we have to simply believe it's there.

We found a community garden by the tracks, emptied of humans
by the threatening rain, the air warming and loamy with a winter
of fallen leaves. As we stepped between beds, you picked

the six-foot skeleton of a sunflower, a drably jubilant
souvenir, wandered the dried plants waiting to be tilled
back to earth—when a killdeer

screeched, sprung
from her nest
and charged us,

her heart surging with threat—
I raised hands, backed away
from her, no bigger than my foot

and brave in the face of a future
which, in some instant curled around ours,
I ended. Four speckled eggs among the decay.

She built her nest on the ground, cared nothing of the mysteries,
the last dramatic cough expelled, gentle fall of the hand to bedspread.
She knows what happens to the throat exposed.

As the clouds finally unfastened, we wove toward a home tucked
safe in the sky and I imagined her sprinting to her pebbled scrape,
fluffing her chest as she settled back down,

leaving open, always,
a dark and tilting eye. I thought
in a thinking I imagined as hers

you get just this one chance
while the maple trees began again
to run their blood, show their little blossoms.

Later, at home, because we had to do something,
you painted a picture of everything you'd seen
existing on one plane of being

while I wrote a bit, then pulled out the bedsheets,
the sewing machine, crafted fabric masks to donate
from a pattern I found online. We had to do something.

And when the old pain finally crashed on me
again, the bolts behind my eyes tightening,
you revealed yourself: the one who knows me

well enough to lay me down at dusk saying,
just relax, enjoy the watermelon,
enjoy the indirect light

laying a ragged quilt
over me against the heat,
its lightness and coolness flushing my skin.

I had been big for so long that I'd forgotten this feeling:
to wrap my arms around my mother's hips,
press my cheek to her belly, gurgling and full of blood.

I pull you in, circle my fingertips around the back of your head,
trace the smooth, hairless scar where you cracked it
on the boat floor while drunk and taking a piss.

Dumb shit like this makes up most of a life.
What would be enough to put in a poem?
What is any of this?

Chris, what am I supposed to tell them?

I talk a big game. The truth: death
is what I fear when I look at you.
To be made alone again. No future
again.

We accept love
now knowing
it will leave us.

I watch the moon and her laughing little face
over your shoulder as you fuck me how I like,
with care and hard and on the couch. Just the three of us tonight.

After, Lou will sing for the hundred-millionth time
about how to hang on and we will unsettle ourselves
into the effervescent crinkling of sheets around our shoulders

like rain fizzing out against the window. Between my ear
and the pillow, my heart's steady echo. And in the morning,
my day will begin again with you, your soft smile when I kiss

the mole on your neck, speckled and elliptic as an egg, when I kiss
the stubble on your cheek and it will hurt and I will wish again that you were
        a woman
but not enough to exchange you. And I will whisper in your ear, just to
        remind you,

to imagine our future is to imagine a world with us in it.

In this final and always morning
there will be no sparrow at the window. Only a crossword in the sun,
a fruit and nut mix for my porridge, a painting never really finished.

We will open toward the new day as the day opens toward us.
A gesture toward what we walk away from,
the empty, shrugging arms of what we walk toward.

Trust

It is Friday morning

and the world is happy to be

nearly through with it.

I am just starting

ever just starting still

in the morning of my life

Notes

In "Forestalled Decomposition for Public Display," the word *denarii* refers to the coins placed on the eyes of deceased Romans to assure safe passage into the underworld.

"Hic Iacet Sepultus" is a Latin phrase which translates to "Here Lies the Body Of," as found on gravestones. *"Verbi Dei Minister"* translates to "Minister of the Word of God." *Muscicapa striata* is the scientific name for the spotted flycatcher.

My practice in the second half of this book (and in my daily life) of referring to all living beings using "they/she/he" pronouns is inspired by Robin Wall Kimmerer's description of the Potawatomi language in her essay "The Grammar of Animacy" from her brilliant collection *Braiding Sweetgrass*. She succinctly explains: "If a maple is an *it*, we can take up the chainsaw. If a maple is a *her*, we think twice."

"Hospice" (page 35) borrows its cyclical concept of time from Kimmerer's essay "In the Footsteps of Nanabozho: Becoming Indigenous to Place" from *Braiding Sweetgrass*.

"I Was Conceived Under a Chemo Moon" borrows the line "Gratitude toward the houseplants, shame/for what they must endure" from the poem "Your News Hour Is Now Two Hours" and the line "[His] order is not our order" from "Mole," both from Karen Solie's *The Road In Is Not the Same Road Out*.

"The Nature Problem" references the poem "Bow River Desk Set" by Liz Howard.

"This Is the Morning of a Meaningless Sparrow at the Window" (page 62) paraphrases the line "She cares nothing about the mystery," from Jack Gilbert's poem "Alone."

"Trust" (page 66) nods, in its final line, to the song "The Morning of Our Lives" by Jonathan Richman & the Modern Lovers.

In Conversation With

This Wound Is a World, Billy-Ray Belcourt

Slow Lightning, Eduardo C. Corral

Be With, Forrest Gander

Faithful and Virtuous Night, Louise Glück

Magdalene, Marie Howe

Braiding Sweetgrass, Robin Wall Kimmerer

A Crow Looked at Me, Mount Eerie

Devotions, Mary Oliver

Duino Elegies, Rainer Maria Rilke

The Road In Is Not the Same Road Out, Karen Solie

Acknowledgements

My deepest gratitude for the lands and Indigenous Peoples of the lands on which this book was written: the Mississaugas of the Credit, Anishinaabeg, Chippewa, Kanièn'kehà:ka, Haudenosaunee, Abenaki, and Huron-Wendat of Tkaronto and Tiohtià:ke; the Îyârhe Nakoda, Tsuut'ina First Nation, Blackfoot Confederacy, Shuswap Nation, Ktunaxa Nation, and Métis Nation of Alberta, Region 3 of Minhrpa; and the Yellowknives Dene First Nation and North Slave Métis in Chief Drygeese territory. The teachings of Indigenous writers, Elders, and educators have been foundational to me in writing this book and, I hope, in becoming a more respectful and humble guest and neighbour.

Thank you to the editors of the publications in which some of these poems first appeared: *The Humber Literary Review, Eavesdrop, The Ampersand Review, PRISM International, Watch Your Head, 30 Under 30: An Anthology of Canadian Millennials, CV2, Vallum Magazine, Arc Poetry Magazine, Forget the Box,* and *The Rusty Toque.*

Thank you to Catriona and Emma at Desert Pets Press for publishing the chapbook *Fourth Walk,* which was, in essence, a trial run of this collection. Thank you to jurors Domenica Martinello, Irfan Ali, and Jacob McArthur Mooney and to the Writers' Trust of Canada for nominating a selection of these poems for the Bronwen Wallace Award for Emerging Writers in 2021.

Thank you to the Toronto Arts Council, Ontario Arts Council, Conseil des arts et des lettres du Québec, Canada Council for the Arts, Social Sciences and Humanities Research Council, Banff Centre for the Arts, and Al and Eurithe Purdy A-Frame Association for granting me the invaluable financial support and time to complete this book.

Thanks to Jay, Hazel, Britt, and Reid at Book*hug Press for their ongoing and undeniable passion in our literary community; I feel so lucky to call you my publisher. To my editor, Jacob McArthur Mooney, for all your support, then and now. Special thanks to Stuart Ross for his astute copy edits, and to Michel Vrana for the wonderful book design. To everyone in my BA and MA creative writing cohorts and to my mentors over the years: David Goldstein, Stephanie Bolster, Karen Solie, Aisha Sasha John, Eduardo C. Corral, and Ariana Reines; I would not have been able to bring this book into the world without your support. Finally, love forever to my dear ones: Alex, Jamie, Liz, Christine, and Erin. And, obviously, Chris. Still.

JESSICA BEBENEK is a queer interdisciplinary poet and educator from Tkaronto (Toronto) who now splits her time between Tiohtià:ke (Montreal) and an off-grid shack on unceded Anishinaabeg territory. She works as a risograph printer and bookmaker at Concordia University's Centre for Expanded Poetics, where she organized the international Occult Poetics Symposium. In 2021, Bebenek was a finalist for the Writers' Trust of Canada Bronwen Wallace Award for Emerging Writers. Her writing has been nominated for the Journey Prize, Pushcart Prize, and CBC Poetry Prize, and she is the author of eight chapbooks, including *I Remember the Exorcism*. *No One Knows Us There* is her first book of poetry.

Colophon

Manufactured as the first edition of
No One Knows Us There
in the spring of 2025 by Book*hug Press

Edited for the press by Jacob McArthur Mooney
Copy-edited by Stuart Ross
Proofread by Hazel Millar
Type + design by Michel Vrana
Cover image: *Still Life with Game, Vegetables, Fruit, and a Cockatoo*
by Adriaen van Utrecht, J. Paul Getty Museum. From Rawpixel.com

Printed in Canada

bookhugpress.ca